W9-AQL-756

Visual Geography Series®

ECUADOR

...in Pictures

Prepared by
Geography Department

Lerner Publications Company
Minneapolis

VISUAL GEOGRAPHY SERIES®

Publisher
Harry Jonas Lerner
Associate Publisher
Nancy M. Campbell
Executive Series Editor
Mary M. Rodgers
Assistant Series Editor
Gretchen Bratvold
Editorial Assistant
Nora W. Kniskern
Illustrations Editors
Nathan A. Haverstock
Karen A. Sirvaitis
Consultants/Contributors
Dr. Ruth F. Hale
Nathan A. Haverstock
Sandra K. Davis
Designer
Jim Simondet
Cartographer
Carol F. Barrett
Indexer
Kristine S. Schubert
Production Manager
Gary J. Hansen

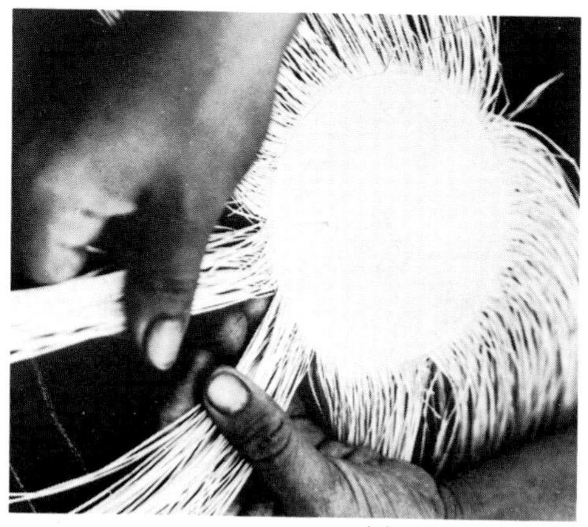

Independent Picture Service

A craftsperson weaves dried jipijapa leaves into a panama hat.

This book is an all-new edition of the Visual Geography Series. Previous editions were published by Sterling Publishing Company, New York City. The text, set in 10/12 Century Textbook, is fully revised and updated, and new photographs, maps, charts, and captions have been added.

Website address: www.lernerbooks.com

LIBRARY OF CONGRESS CATALOGING-IN-PUBLICATION DATA

Ecuador in pictures.

(Visual geography series)
Rev. ed. of: Ecuador in pictures / prepared by Martha Murray Sumwalt.
Includes index.
Summary: Text and photographs introduce the geography, history, economy, culture, and people of the South American country whose name derives from the equator.
1. Ecuador. [1. Ecuador] I. Sumwalt, Martha Murray. Ecuador in pictures. II. Lerner Publications Company. Geography Dept. III. Series: Visual geography series (Minneapolis, Minn.)
F3708.E384 1987 986.6 87-3956
ISBN 0-8225-1813-9 (lib. bdg.)

International Standard Book Number: 0-8225-1813-9
Library of Congress Catalog Card Number: 87-3956

Independent Picture Service

Rope sellers wearing traditional hats and shawls stretch out their wares for sale.

Acknowledgments

Title page photo by Robert E. Olson.

Elevation contours adapted from *The Times Atlas of the World,* seventh comprehensive edition (New York: Times Books, 1985).

5 6 7 8 9 10 - JR - 03 02 01 00 99 98

Photo by William Gualtieri

In the coastal lowlands, where seasonal rains cause frequent flooding, residents build their houses on stilts.

Contents

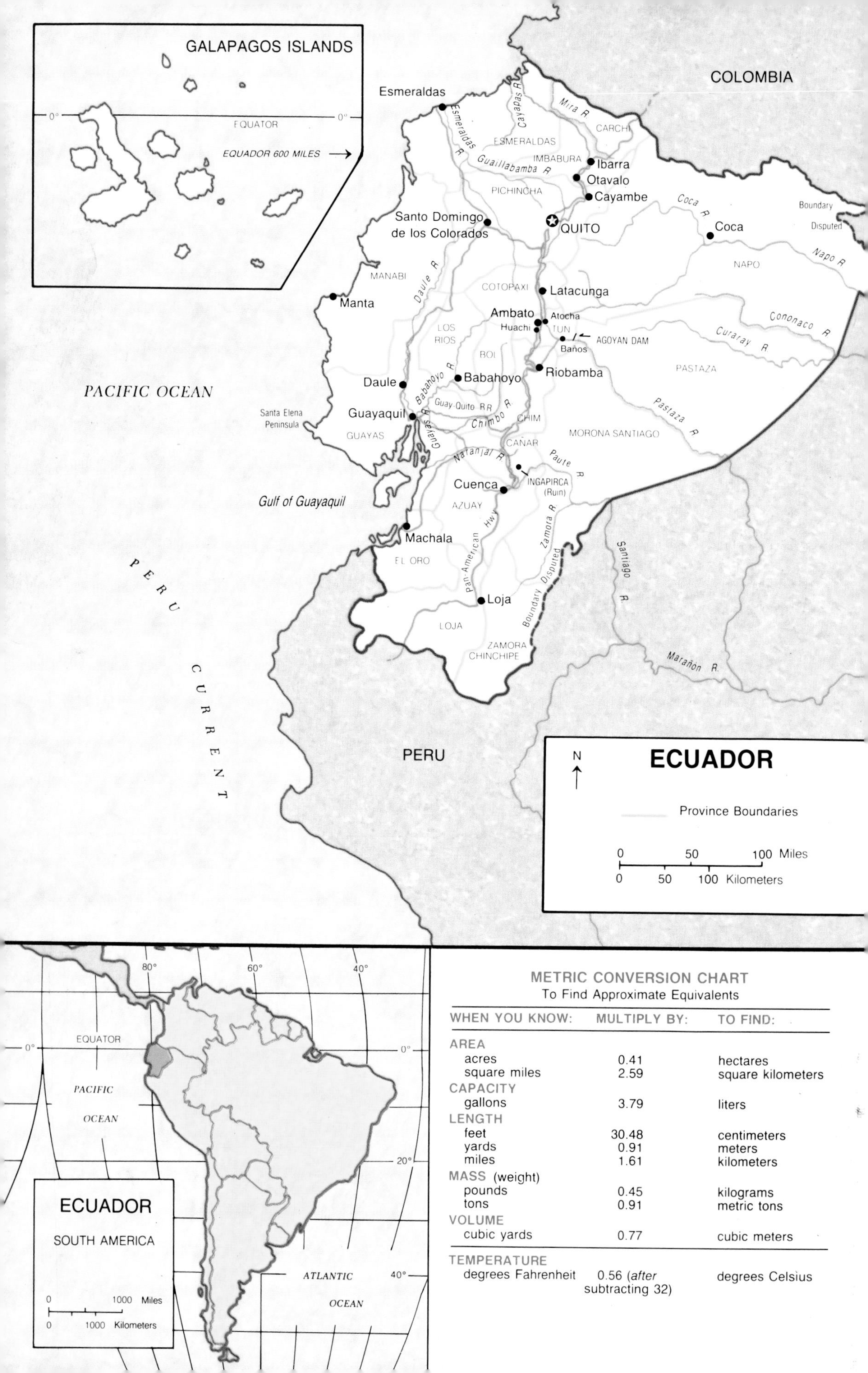

METRIC CONVERSION CHART

To Find Approximate Equivalents

WHEN YOU KNOW:	MULTIPLY BY:	TO FIND:
AREA		
acres	0.41	hectares
square miles	2.59	square kilometers
CAPACITY		
gallons	3.79	liters
LENGTH		
feet	30.48	centimeters
yards	0.91	meters
miles	1.61	kilometers
MASS (weight)		
pounds	0.45	kilograms
tons	0.91	metric tons
VOLUME		
cubic yards	0.77	cubic meters
TEMPERATURE		
degrees Fahrenheit	0.56 (*after* subtracting 32)	degrees Celsius

Courtesy of Leonard Soroka

This section of the Andean oil pipeline – essential to the export of Ecuador's petroleum deposits – ruptured during an earthquake in 1987.

Introduction

Most of Ecuador's early inhabitants lived in the mountainous highlands. After the Spanish conquest, even newcomers from the Old World settled either in the mountains or in the coastal lowlands near the Pacific Ocean. During many centuries, the jungle to the east of the Andes, called El Oriente (the East), figured in Ecuador's popular imagination as a far-off place that held sources of fabulous wealth.

That myth became reality in 1967 when Texaco and Gulf oil companies discovered vast petroleum deposits in El Oriente. To get the oil out of the jungle, the companies constructed the world's highest pipeline. The pipeline climbed up and over the Andes and down to the hot, humid tropical coast at Esmeraldas, where tankers waited to pick up the oil.

Oil began to flow in the 1970s—precisely when world oil prices were at their all-time peak. With the pipeline in operation, Ecuador pumped 300,000 barrels a day. Revenues reached an unbelievable $270 million per month.

Because of Ecuador's sudden oil bonanza, the government began to subsidize the cost of living in Ecuador. Low prices were decreed for nearly everything, and oil profits made up the difference in cost.

Clearly, however, not all Ecuadorans shared equally in the oil profits. A small minority who participated in oil-related activities was able to line its pockets with oil revenues. The lucky few included government officials—whose approval was required to sustain the flow of oil—and those involved in actual oil production, such as manual laborers.

Lawyers, accountants, and businesspeople—whose services or supplies were needed to insure the performance of the oil sector—jumped on the oil bandwagon. Even officers of the armed forces got involved by organizing the troops to protect the oil from real or imagined threats.

When oil prices dropped, however, Ecuadorans were forced once again to face the consequences of a troubled past, including a history of corrupt and unsettled governments. During Ecuador's first 95 years as an independent nation, it had a succession of 40 presidents, dictators, and military juntas. Few leaders were in office long enough to address national needs. From 1925 to 1948, none of the 22 chiefs of state completed the term of office decreed by law.

The presidents who have ruled Ecuador since August of 1979—when Ecuador returned to an elected civilian government—have confronted difficult tasks. Popular discontent has arisen because of sharp drops in the country's oil earnings.

The people may face even greater economic problems by the early twenty-first century, when Ecuador's oil reserves are expected to run dry. Public confidence in the government's ability to handle Ecuador's economic problems has declined steadily.

Many Ecuadorans now view oil as a questionable blessing. Nevertheless, Ecuadorans are also trying to protect their fragile democracy and to develop the full range of their resources. The people hope their efforts will improve the country's standard of living—a goal that has eluded Ecuadorans for centuries.

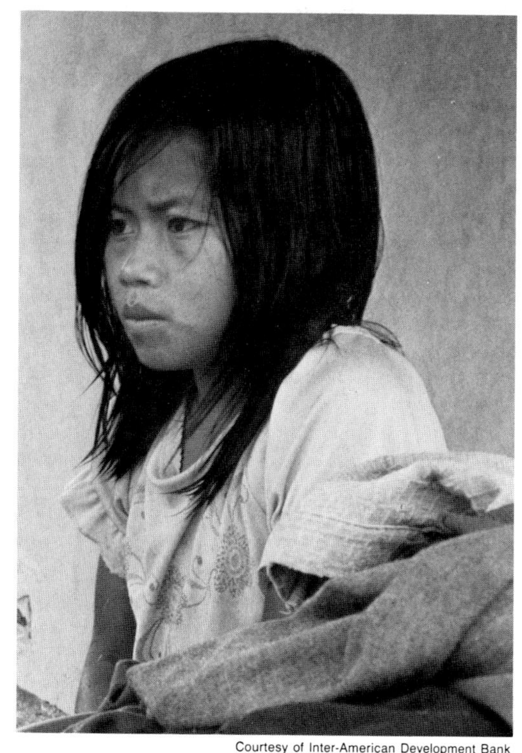

Courtesy of Inter-American Development Bank

Poverty still exists in Ecuador, despite the oil profits, which have not reached all citizens equally.

Photo by Doris Rubenstein

Along the road between Santo Domingo de los Colorados and Quito, a granite statue carved into a sheer rock hillside reminds passersby that the area is famous for its natural traffic hazards. The legend on the statue translates as "The Brutal Power."

Courtesy of Evangeline Quam

Sally Lightfoot crabs jump in the crevices between rock formations, and marine iguanas—the world's only seaworthy lizards—sun themselves on the rugged Galápagos Islands.

1) The Land

The Republic of Ecuador, on the west coast of South America between Colombia and Peru, is crossed by the equator, from which the nation takes its Spanish name. With 109,484 square miles of territory, Ecuador is about equal in size to the state of Nevada.

Ecuador's rugged topography comprises coastal lowlands, towering Andean mountains, and tropical jungles of the Amazon Basin. Offshore, at a distance of 600 miles from the mainland, Ecuador's territory also includes the Galápagos Islands. Nineteenth-century British naturalist Charles Darwin documented the Galápagos's rich plant and animal life, from which he developed his theory of the evolution of life on earth. Scientists from many nations still frequent the islands today to study flora and fauna that have evolved under unique environmental conditions.

Topography

THE COSTA

The *costa* is a 20- to 100-mile-wide strip of lowlands that lies between the Andes and the Pacific Ocean. Near Guayaquil—the costa's and the nation's biggest city—a range of hills interrupts the flatness of the lowlands. For thousands of years, Andean

Photo by Dr. Ellen Ordway

In the crisp mountain air of north central Ecuador, the snow-covered peak of Mount Cotopaxi is clearly visible.

rivers have dumped rich volcanic ash in the costa. The soil eventually was carried to the large delta at the mouth of the Guayas River. This fertile lowland area has become the most commercially productive region of the nation.

THE SIERRA

Moving eastward from the Pacific lowlands, Ecuador's land rises toward the Andes, or sierra, which encompass about one-quarter of the nation's total area. The Andean section that passes through Ecuador is called the Cordillera Real (Royal Range). It has two chains that run north to south through the length of the country. Between these ranges—which are joined in several places by horizontal ridges—lie fertile valleys that are occupied by more than one-half of Ecuador's people.

High mountain peaks dot the landscape. Chimborazo at 20,561 feet is the tallest,

Courtesy of Jeannine Bayard

Streams flow and vegetation thrives in the lush jungles of El Oriente.

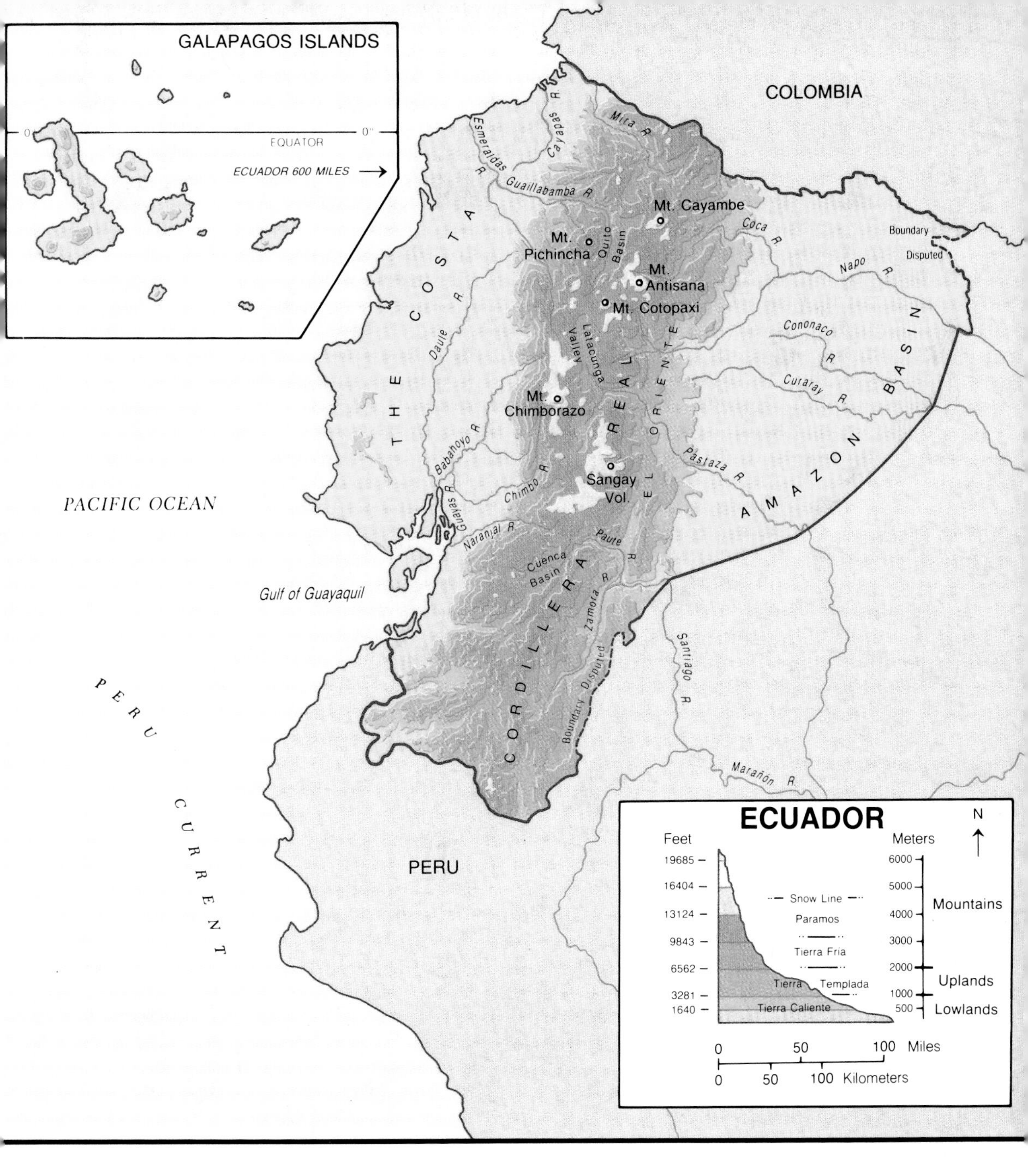

followed by Cotopaxi—the world's highest active volcano—Cayambe, Antisana, and Sangay.

EL ORIENTE

Beginning at the eastern foothills of the Andes and extending to the Amazon Basin, El Oriente is made up of rain-forests, jungles, and rivers. Upon entering this region from the highlands, the altitude drops rapidly, and waterfalls and mighty rapids carry water along cold mountaintops. Lower down, at about 850 feet above sea level, the land is more level and, when cleared, is better suited to farming. About half of Ecuador is covered by dense jungles that have already revealed enormous petroleum deposits east of the Andes. Moreover, the jungles have tremendous future potential for agricultural purposes.

The Galápagos Islands

This group of volcanic islands 600 miles west of the mainland was discovered in 1535 by Tomás de Berlanga, a Spanish explorer. At first, they were called Las Islas Encantadas (the Enchanted Islands) because of the area's strong currents, which often deceived navigators. Later they were named the Galápagos (Spanish for turtles) for the giant tortoises discovered there. Uninhabited for centuries, the islands were taken over by Ecuador in 1832.

Because of the popularity of the islands with British pirates, navigators, and naturalists, the individual landmasses soon acquired English as well as Spanish names. Alexander Selkirk, the model for Robinson Crusoe, visited the islands in 1709 after being rescued by British pirates from Más a Tierra off the coast of Chile. In *Las Encantadas,* writer Herman Melville described his visit to the Galápagos on a whaling ship. Darwin visited the islands in 1835 and recorded his journey in *The Zoology of the Voyage of the Beagle.* He called the islands a "living laboratory of evolution." After Charles William Beebe's *Galápagos, World's End* was published in 1923, small groups of immigrants came to live on the islands.

Rivers

Ecuador is crisscrossed by many streams and rivers. Several saltwater passages encroach upon coastal lands from the Pacific Ocean. The Guayas River, which drains the lower western region, has many tributaries, the largest of which are the Daule, Babahoyo, Chimbo, and Naranjal rivers. Within about 50 miles, eight rivers pour into the Gulf of Guayaquil and empty huge amounts of fresh water into the Pacific. In the northwest the Mira, Cayapas, and Esmeraldas rivers all flow to the Pacific. A tributary of the Esmeraldas drains the Quito Basin and passes through a gorge in the Cordillera Real.

South of the capital city of Quito lies the Latacunga Valley, which is drained by the Pastaza River on its southeastward route to the Amazon. Farther south, the Santiago River (called the Zamora in Ecuador) drains the Cuenca Basin before joining the Marañón and later the Amazon.

Major rivers in El Oriente are the Coca, Napo, Curaray, and Cononaco, all of which also flow into the Amazon. Ecuadorans often lament the fact that navigable portions of the Amazon lie just 50 miles outside of Ecuador's territory—in neighboring Peru.

Courtesy of Leonard Soroka

Galápagos turtles are found nowhere else but on the volcanic islands named after them. Like most of the Galápagos animals, the tortoises exhibit no fear of humans and are unusually tame.

The 400-mile-long Pastaza River rises in central Ecuador, flows south to Peru, and eventually empties into the Marañón – a major headstream of the Amazon.

Courtesy of Jeannine Bayard

A cloud-dotted view of the Guaillabamba River shows its curved course and heavily sedimented waters. This waterway, which flows north of Quito, is one of the larger tributaries of the Esmeraldas River.

Courtesy of Leonard Soroka

Climate

Similar to the climate of other mountainous countries that are located in the tropics, temperatures in Ecuador vary with elevation. Rainfall depends on exposure to rain-bearing winds, and changes in climate are often abrupt. While most of the sierra gets plenty of rain, a dry area just north of Quito receives very little rain at all. Southern Ecuador and the Santa Elena Peninsula west of Guayaquil are also arid.

At low elevations in the coastal and eastern areas, temperatures generally average between 75° and 78° F. El Oriente has a typically hot equatorial climate, with no low temperatures and none higher than 100° F. Rainfall usually exceeds 80 inches annually and sometimes reaches 200 inches in the rain-forest.

Ecuador's northwestern coast tends to be warm and wet, while its southwestern coast is drier. Immediately south of Esmeraldas, the rainy season occurs between January and May, but farther south this season grows shorter. The Peru Current, which flows out of the southern Pacific Ocean from June to December, cools coastal waters and also causes heavy fog.

Farther inland, the climate varies with altitude. The tierra caliente, or hot zone, extends from sea level to about 3,000 feet. From 3,000 to 6,500 feet is the tierra templada, or moderately warm region. Above this level is the tierra fría, or cold land, which extends to over 10,000 feet. The windy, treeless paramos (alpine plateaus) are found at a still-higher level. The highest climatic level of all is the snow line, found at about 15,000 feet above sea level.

Not surprisingly, each altitude has developed specially adapted crops and different land uses. Bananas and cacao are found at the lower elevations, coffee and beans are grown in the tierra templada, and potatoes thrive in the tierra fría. The paramos are often used as grazing land for sheep and goats.

Very little seasonal variation occurs between the warmest and the coldest months within each of these climatic zones. In Quito, for example, January temperatures average 56° F while August temperatures average 57° F.

Courtesy of John H. Peck

A tall tree in the Ecuadoran rain-forest plays host to clinging epiphytes, which use the tree for support but take their nutrients and moisture from the air.

Flora and Fauna

South America contains an unusual combination of plant and animal life, including species found in North America and many varieties that are native only to the southern continent. Isolated jungles, valleys, and mountains, as well as wide variations of climate, account for Ecuador's enormous assortment of flora and fauna.

FLORA

The wet lowlands and rain-forests of the tierra caliente on the coast and in El Oriente contain over 2,000 species of plants, including ferns, palms, bamboo, and tropical fruits. Many plants are entangled with thick vines, called lianas, which root in the ground and climb up around tree trunks. Such vines can eventually strangle the host plant with their octopuslike tentacles. Epiphytes—mosses, lichens, and orchids, for example—grow on other plants but get their moisture and nutrients from the air.

Leaves of the jipijapa tree are used to weave straw panama hats and are found in Ecuador's northwestern coastal forests. Vegetable ivory, from which buttons and other ornaments are carved, comes from the seeds of the native tagua tree. Thriving along tropical river banks are giant bamboo trees, which sometimes reach 60 feet in height and which are used for building houses along the coast.

Many familiar fruits—such as oranges, lemons, grapefruits, coconuts, apricots, papayas, and pomegranates—are found in

Courtesy of Museum of Modern Art of Latin America

The dried leaves of the jipijapa tree are braided by hand to make panama hats, so called because the hats were sold to people in transit across the Isthmus of Panama.

Courtesy of Earl H. Lubensky

A 450-foot-wide waterhole in the savanna southwest of Guayaquil shows the lush effects of the area's heavy seasonal rains.

Independent Picture Service

Capybaras grow to about four feet in length and can weigh as much as 100 pounds. Largest of the world's rodents, capybaras are semi-aquatic animals that swim along the banks of rivers and lakes and feed on nearby vegetation.

the warm regions of Ecuador. But more unusual types also grow in the nation. For example, the flesh of the cherimoya fruit tastes like strawberry, pineapple, and banana combined. The naranjilla, a small yellow fruit, has a distinctive flavor midway between a peach and an orange. The mammee has a soft, red pulp contained in a hard rind, while the pepino is a purple-and-white fruit that resembles a cucumber.

FAUNA

The widest variety of Ecuador's animal life is in the rain-forests. Jaguars, ocelots, porcupines, and monkeys find homes in the jungle. Both the peccary—a wild, piglike creature with sharp tusks—and the odd-looking tapir feed on plants and move about at night. Although llamas, vicuñas, and alpacas are not as numerous in Ecuador as they are in Peru, they are herded, and some Indians in the southern sierra make rugs and garments from their wool.

Busy anteaters use their long noses and tongues to poke around in anthills and rotten wood, and burrowing armadillos roll up in their hard, scaly shells when frightened. The world's largest rodent—the pig-sized capybara—flees to the lakes and streams when in danger.

While Ecuador is the winter home of many North American birds, it also has a wide variety of native winged creatures. Flitting through Ecuador's forests are bright-feathered parrots, macaws, cotingas, and jacamars. Jungle noisemakers include the horned screamer, trumpeter bird, and white-crested bellbird, whose startled cry sounds like the clap of a bell. Ecuadoran skies are filled with hawks, falcons, and vultures. Condors, whose image appears on Ecuador's national seal, are found in the Andes. Scientist Alexander von Humboldt watched condors circling over Chimborazo at an altitude of over 23,000 feet. Charles Darwin recorded that he saw a condor sail in the air for more than half an hour without once moving its 10-foot wingspan.

FLORA AND FAUNA OF THE GALAPAGOS

The flora and fauna of the Galápagos Islands have long attracted natural scientists. These scientists claim that 97 percent of the reptiles, 47 percent of the plants, and 37 percent of the fish living in the waters of this particular archipelago can be found nowhere else on the globe. Darwin noticed that animals of the Galápagos—although they were of the same species as those that

Courtesy of Leonard Soroka

Friendly sea lions bask in the sun on the Galápagos Islands. These seals thrive throughout the islands and take their nourishment from the abundance of marine life.

Courtesy of Leonard Soroka

Plentiful iguanas live the more typical lifestyles of land-based reptiles than do their relatives, the seaweed-eating marine iguanas. Both species inhabit the Galápagos Islands, though the marine variety is found nowhere else in the world.

lived on the mainland—had developed special characteristics in order to survive in their isolated environment. For instance, because food was hard to reach, Galápagos tortoises had longer necks, and finches on the islands had differently shaped beaks. Darwin used these observations to document his theory of evolution in *The Origin of Species*.

Seals and penguins swim the Peru Current as it moves northward off Ecuador's coast and reaches the equatorial waters surrounding the Galápagos. The giant iguanas described by Darwin are still found, but the huge native turtles—some weighing as much as 500 pounds—face extinction because of earlier hunters. Other unusual Galápagos creatures are the short-eared owl, the blue-footed booby, and the bump-headed titmouse. Unable to fly, the cormorants of the archipelago stand about on the beaches, flap their short wings, and croak.

Courtesy of Leonard Soroka

The blue-footed booby—so named because of the bright blue shade of its webbed feet—is one of the rare birds found on the Galápagos Islands.

Cities and Towns

Although Ecuador is a small country, marked contrasts in climate and elevation have combined to distinguish the settings of its towns and regions. Coastal cities bear little resemblance to those of the sierra, and El Oriente has a frontier character all its own. The rush of people to inhabit the cities has created slums—areas of makeshift housing where services are scarce—but both Quito and Guayaquil are trying to solve this problem with low-cost housing projects.

GUAYAQUIL

Guayaquil (officially called Santiago de Guayaquil), population 1.5 million, is Ecuador's largest city. This bustling port is located in the humid tropics on the banks of the Guayas River, about 40 miles east of the Pacific Ocean. The traffic of the Guayas—one of Ecuador's busiest waterways—includes many kinds of boats, from dugout canoes and balsa rafts to huge

Photo by Amandus Schneider

The twin towers of Guayaquil's cathedral jut into the sky and are a distinctive part of the cityscape.

Courtesy of Inter-American Development Bank

Ecuadoran authorities have undertaken extensive landfill and sewage projects to benefit slum areas of Guayaquil, which often suffer flooding from seasonal rains.

freighters and passenger ships. Guayaquil's modern port facilities have helped to make it an important shipping hub that handles most of Ecuador's international trade.

GUAYAQUIL-QUITO RAILROAD

A railway completed at great cost early in the twentieth century links Guayaquil and Quito, two cities that have been rivals since the Spanish conquest of the sixteenth century. Though the long journey inland from Guayaquil can be tiring, the train crosses spectacular terrain and affords breathtaking vistas of mountain scenery. After traveling 50 miles across the lowlands, the rail line climbs rapidly to Nariz de Diable (Devil's Nose)—a double zigzag that has been cut out of solid rock.

QUITO

Quito, the Ecuadoran capital city, lies at the opposite end of the railway journey from Guayaquil. The capital has a population of 1.1 million people and is located

Courtesy of Earl H. Lubensky

Rivers and hills flash by the train windows along the route of the Guayaquil-Quito Railroad. Heavy rains in 1983 washed away important sections of track and canceled several stops.

Photo by Dr. Ellen Ordway

Lying high in the Andes Mountains, Quito occupies a large basin—a piece of level ground surrounded by highlands. The capital has greatly expanded in the twentieth century.

Courtesy of Earl H. Lubensky

Cuenca's cathedral faces Parque Calderón amid buildings of various hues made from the locally quarried marble.

Courtesy of Laurie Nelsen

On Cerro Panecillo just outside Quito a statue entitled the Virgen de las Américas overlooks the capital.

at an elevation of 9,000 feet on the rim of the Pichincha Basin. Few cities have a more beautiful setting than Quito—the second highest capital in the world, after La Paz in Bolivia. Founded by the Spanish in 1534 on the ruins of an Incan city, Quito is one of the most historic and picturesque capitals in the Western Hemisphere. The city is famous for its colonial-era art found in more than 100 churches, chapels, convents, and monasteries.

About 15 miles north of Quito is a monument marking the equator. Charles-Marie de La Condamine and his French scientific expedition established the line in 1735. The Solar Museum near the equator contains information about the cult of the sun, which was important to pre-Columbian Indians.

SECONDARY CITIES

Cuenca (population 195,000), located 200 miles south of Quito, is a living museum of Ecuadoran history. Over 450 years ago, the Incan emperor Huayna Capac built the town of Tomebamba on the site as a rest stop on the mountain road from Cuzco in southern Peru to Quito. He also constructed a fortress at nearby Ingapirca. In 1557, on the foundations of Tomebamba, the Spaniards began to build Cuenca. The cobblestone streets and red-tiled roofs left by the Spanish remind visitors of Cuenca's colonial history.

A new highway has revolutionized the lives of the residents of Santo Domingo de los Colorados, located about 80 mountainous miles west of Quito. Until the highway's completion, the town was known as the home of the Colorado (red) Indians, who rub acid into their hair to give it a distinctive, reddish color. Santo Domingo's fortunes are booming because of its location at the junction of all-weather roads leading to Quito and to such commercially important coastal cities as Manta and Guayaquil. Santo Domingo is also a center for the commercial processing of crops that are important in Ecuador's trade with the world.

Courtesy of Minneapolis Public Library and Information Center

Few of the Colorado Indians dress traditionally today. Their reddened hair and brightly colored clothing at one time distinguished them among Ecuador's various native groups.

Courtesy of Museum of Modern Art of Latin America

A statue with expressive eyes, large nostrils, and a rectangular mouth is from the pre-Columbian, Jama-Coaque culture dating from 200 B.C. to A.D. 500.

2) History and Government

For centuries, the area now occupied by Ecuador was known as the kingdom of Quito, named after the Quitus Indians who lived in the region. According to archaeologists, pre-Columbian Ecuador hosted a combination of peoples who spoke a Chibchan dialect. Similarities in the dress, crafts, and speech of the various Indians in Colombia, Panama, and northwestern Ecuador lead some historians to suspect a common heritage.

Pre-Columbian Era

Ecuador's coastal Indians were mostly hunters and fishermen who traded their goods using dugout canoes and large balsa rafts with sails. They exchanged salt, fish, parrots, monkeys, and achiote (seeds that yield a dye) for cloth, blankets, and precious metals possessed by the highland Indians. With the exception of the Cayapa and the Colorado, these coastal Indians either disappeared or intermarried with other races.

Although Ecuador's pre-Columbian tribes spoke different languages, they shared many customs. Even after being conquered by the Incas in the fourteenth century, the local groups still retained their cultural identities. For example, small estates continued to be ruled by powerful chieftains who were allowed to have many wives. Similar to Incan communities, however, class differences were emphasized by the ornate clothes and jewels worn by people of the noble class.

Most highland Indians farmed small parcels of land on which they raised beans, squash, maize (corn), potatoes, and quinoa, (a pigweed whose seeds were used as grain). They lived in wood-framed, mud-plastered houses with thatched roofs and had domesticated animals, including dogs and guinea pigs. Their clothing usually consisted of long, sleeveless shirts or wrap-around skirts, with shoulder blankets for warmth.

Because the local tribes were often hostile toward one another, the men were often at war. Consequently, the women did much of the farm work. When the men were not fighting, they wove textiles, carved tools, and made weapons of metal or stone.

Nature had an important place in Indian religions, which included numerous spirits. Shamans, or priests, acted as spokespeople between the Indians and their gods. The coastal Indians, who worshipped the sea, fish, snakes, pumas, and jaguars, built richly decorated totem poles, some of which were 40 feet in height. Typically, a totem was carved with alternating male and female figures, arranged in sequence from childhood to maturity.

Independent Picture Service

The stone of the 12 angles illustrates the legendary skill of Incan stone masons.

The Incan Conquest

Ecuador's Indians were the last tribes to be subdued by the Incas before the arrival of the Spaniards. These local groups never were thoroughly integrated into the structure of the Inca Empire. Even after conquering the Ecuadoran Indians, the Incas were forced to make concessions to control them—such as maintaining the traditional privileges of the conquered chieftains.

During roughly 100 years of Incan rule in Ecuador, the Incas built roads, brought in new crops and animals, and introduced the Quechua language. The mountain road from Cuzco, the southern Incan capital, to Quito, the main city of the northern provinces, was 1,250 miles long. *Chasquis*—relay runners who carried messages from one part of the empire to another—could run this distance in five days. Since they had no written language, the Indians used

Photo by Organization of American States

Born in about 1502 to the Lord Inca Huayna Capac and a Quito princess, Atahuallpa became the undisputed leader—and the last ruler—of the Inca Empire in 1530.

Courtesy of Earl H. Lubensky

Ingapirca is Ecuador's only major Incan ruin. Although it is called a fortress, the complex of buildings is more likely to have been used for religious ceremonies than for defense.

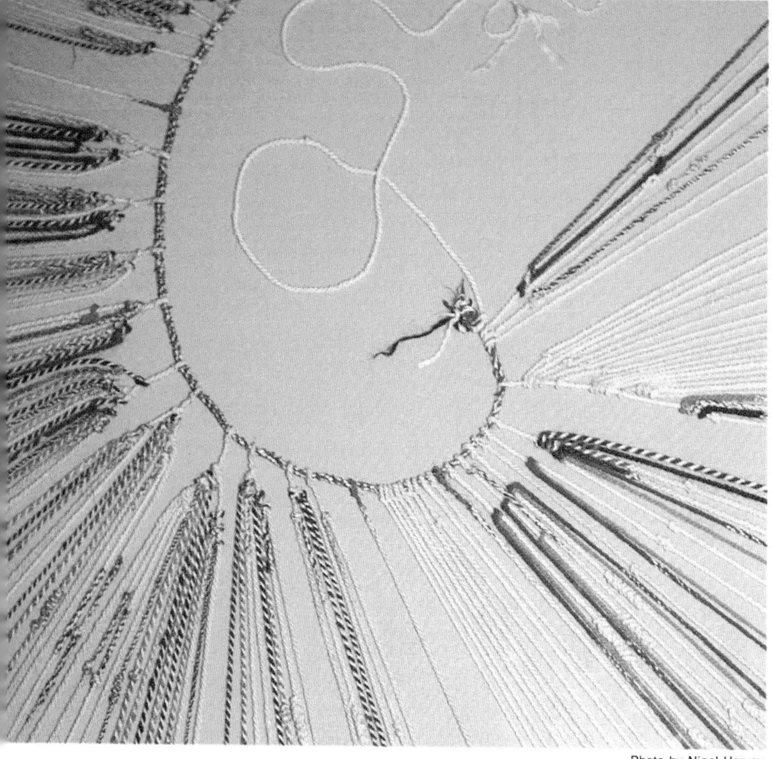

Photo by Nigel Harvey

The Incas used quipus–or knotted strings–to keep records and introduced this system to the conquered Indians of Ecuador. The length, thickness, color, and number of knots on a given string indicated a variety of important information. For example, white and yellow strings kept track respectively of silver and gold supplies.

quipus (knotted strings) to keep records and to send messages.

Indians were divided into *ayllus,* or clans, comprised of people who lived together and shared the land for cultivating crops. Common Incas paid taxes in the form of service to the Lord Inca by laboring on imperial farms, in state mines, or as part of work crews that constructed roads, bridges, forts, and temples.

While the Lord Inca Huayna Capac was making a tour of his northern domain in about 1525, he received news that chasquis had sighted two strange ships along the coast. Rumors that these strangers represented a powerful civilization alarmed the Incan ruler, who saw omens of an approaching struggle.

Soon after the sighting of the Spanish ships, Huayna Capac died at his home in Tomebamba (now Cuenca) without naming an heir to his empire. After his death a bloody war broke out between two of Huayna Capac's sons. Eventually, Atahuallpa, the popular son who lived in the northern part of the realm, defeated and killed his half-brother—Cuzco-born Huáscar—and became ruler of the entire Incan territory.

Courtesy of Earl H. Lubensky

The Incan general Rumiñahui attempted to resist the Spanish with a force of 10,000 Incan warriors. His efforts failed, but he ordered the leveling of Quito to spare it from Spanish domination. He was captured and executed by the Spaniards in 1535.

Exploration and Spanish Conquest

In 1526 Bartolomé Ruiz, who had left Panama in one of Francisco Pizarro's ships to explore the lands to the south, visited the Indians near Esmeraldas. He noticed that their leaders wore gold, silver, and emeralds. After collecting a variety of samples, he returned to Panama and reported his findings.

Pizarro himself arrived from Panama in 1532 and arranged to meet Atahuallpa, the new Lord Inca, in Cajamarca, a spa north of Loja. Taking full advantage of Incan disunity due to the empire's recent civil war, Pizarro imprisoned the Incan leader with the help of firearms, which were superior to Incan weapons. Offering the Spaniards a ransom for his freedom, Atahuallpa suggested that his subjects fill three rooms with gold and silver. When Pizarro accepted the offer, the emperor issued the order, and the precious metals began to flow to Cajamarca.

With the gold in hand and believing there was nothing more to be gained by releasing Atahuallpa, Pizarro faithlessly had the Lord Inca killed. The Spaniard justified the deed by calling it revenge for Atahuallpa's earlier murder of Huáscar. When the Incas received word of their emperor's death, warfare broke out between the Incas and the Spaniards. But the virtually leaderless Inca Empire soon fell apart, and the Spaniards eventually moved in to assert their control.

The northern territory of the Inca Empire—still called Quito—was not completely conquered until 1534. After suffering severe losses near Riobamba, Rumiñahui, one of Atahuallpa's most able generals, withdrew to the city of Quito and ordered that the settlement be burned. Finding the former Incan center of power in ashes,

Sebastián de Belalcázar founded San Francisco de Quito on the site in December of 1534.

Colonial Days

In 1539 Francisco Pizarro named his half brother Gonzalo governor of Quito. The younger Pizarro's appetite was aroused by legends of El Dorado (the golden one), a land said to be rich in gold, cinnamon, and other spices. Gonzalo Pizarro organized an expedition from Quito in 1541 to search for these riches in the eastern jungle—now called El Oriente. Pizarro, Francisco de Orellana, and a large group of men traveled across the eastern Andes to the Coca River, where they built light boats to continue their expedition farther east into the jungle.

Sent ahead to find food, Orellana's boat was swept into the Napo River and continued to the Amazon River. Legend relates that, during his trip down this gigantic river to the Atlantic Ocean, Orellana and his crew were attacked by a group of warrior women whom they called "las Amazonas." Although Orellana did not find the fabled land of gold and spices, his discovery of the mighty Amazon brought him great rewards and acclaim in Spain.

PIZARRO'S REVOLT

While Gonzalo Pizarro ruled in Quito, the king of Spain had appointed Blasco Núñez Vela as viceroy in Peru to the south. En route to Lima, the Peruvian capital, Núñez Vela made an unscheduled stop in Quito. He found a revolt in progress led by Pizarro, who was continuing to

Independent Picture Service

Widespread exploitation of the Indians–here being forced by the Spanish conquistadors to pan for gold–eventually eliminated the native population.

Following the founding of the bishopric of Quito, religious buildings—such as the monastery dedicated to Quito's patron saint, San Francisco—were quickly established.

Courtesy of Museum of Modern Art of Latin America

exploit the Indian population—contrary to the wishes of the Spanish government. Núñez Vela, who had been empowered by Spain to protect the Indian groups, organized troops to fight Pizarro. Quito's rebellious colonists killed Núñez Vela in 1546. Pizarro's early success in ruling Quito independently came to an end when Spanish troops defeated his forces in 1548. Another representative of the Spanish crown, Pedro de la Gasca, succeeded in defeating and assassinating Pizarro that same year.

Despite official protection of the Indians, Spain's exploitation continued. Indians were forced to work as slaves for their Spanish masters, who bought and sold these native peoples as part of large agricultural estates. The Indians were easy prey for their exploiters. Under Incan rule, all needs were cared for by the state, thus there was little interest in acquiring wealth. Accustomed to working on communal projects in exchange for their keep, the Indians under Spanish rule were suddenly left to their own devices in fulfilling their needs. The Spaniards replaced the Lord Inca but not the Incan system. They set the Indians to work tilling the land or building churches and governmental structures without providing anything in return.

THE AUDIENCIA OF QUITO

To more easily convert the Indians to Roman Catholic beliefs and to serve the religious needs of the colonists, the bishopric of Quito was established in 1545. Spain recognized Quito's cultural progress in 1563 by elevating the area to the larger administrative status of an audiencia. Under the Spanish hierarchy, however, Quito

Independent Picture Service

The main facade of the Jesuit church of La Compañía in Quito displays heavily carved columns and deep niches to hold religious statues.

still belonged to the even larger Viceroyalty of Peru.

For the next 200 years the Audiencia of Quito experienced the mixed advantages of Spanish-imposed peace. The Spaniards introduced the cultivation of wheat and brought in domesticated animals, such as pigs, sheep, cattle, horses, and donkeys. Also imported, however, were black slaves from Africa to work on sugarcane plantations along the coast where there were few Indians.

From the colonial point of view, there was steady progress throughout settled areas of the audiencia. The city of Quito enjoyed renown as a center of artistic production, and its churches and public buildings were considered among the finest creations of Spanish colonial architecture in the New World.

Independence

It was not until late in the eighteenth century that self-satisfied Quito showed signs of a desire for independence. Chief among the reasons for discontent was a system imposed by Spain on all its colonies whereby the highest posts in the audiencia were reserved for those of Spanish birth. Inspired by the successful wars of independence in France and the United States, Quito saw its own chance for freedom when Spanish power weakened because of Napoleon's invasion of Spain.

There were uprisings in Quito in 1809 and 1810, which were stirred by discontented Creoles—those of Spanish bloodlines born in the colony but excluded from high office. Though attempts to revolt failed, the desire for independence continued to gain momentum until 1821.

Venezuelan-born Simon Bolívar is called "the Liberator" for his role in independence struggles of many present-day South American nations. After securing Venezuela's freedom from Spain, Bolívar headed across the Andes for New Granada (Colombia) and defeated the Spanish forces assembled at Boyacá in 1819. The Battle of Pichincha in 1822 brought the promise of eventual self-government to Ecuador.

Courtesy of Inter-American Development Bank

In that year, the armies of two South American liberators, Simon Bolívar and José Francisco de San Martín, met on the audiencia's territory. On May 24, 1822, General Antonio José de Sucre, Bolívar's most-trusted subordinate, led a rebel army to victory over Spain at the Battle of Pichincha near Quito. This battle is marked as the beginning of Ecuador's independence, though the nation was still far from being able to exercise self-government. The two liberators, Bolívar and San Martín, met again at Guayaquil late in 1822. San Martín agreed to withdraw entirely

Independent Picture Service

José Francisco de San Martín *(above)* and Antonio José de Sucre *(right)* had leading roles in the nineteenth-century armies of South American liberation.

Independent Picture Service

from this campaign for independence and to leave the field to Bolívar. Bolívar incorporated the former Audiencia of Quito into the republic of Gran Colombia (Great Colombia) to fulfill his idea of a union of South American republics that would stretch from Panama to Bolivia.

When Bolívar died in 1830, there was no one on the scene with sufficient experience to maintain his vision. Like other territories of the republic, therefore, Quito seceded from the union. The new nation renamed itself Ecuador (Spanish for equator) and began its existence as a separate country.

Independent Picture Service

The former colony of Quito took Ecuador as its new national name – a reference to the presence within its territory of the equator, the imaginary line that divides the earth into northern and southern halves.

The Early Days of the Republic

Juan José Flores, a Venezuelan-born general and hero of Ecuador's war of independence, dominated Ecuador's first 15 years as a nation. A conservative who represented the interests of the city of Quito, Flores oversaw the adoption of a national constitution and his own election as Ecuador's first president. Conflicts with Guayaquil's citizens, who held more liberal views, forced Flores from power in 1845. In exile in Europe, Flores drummed up support for a comeback, which failed.

Turbulent years lay ahead for Ecuador. Frequent civil disturbances occurred, and border conflicts erupted with Peru and Colombia. Between 1845 and 1860, Ecuador was ruled by 11 presidents and several military juntas. During this period local leaders were wary of giving up their independence in order to establish a strong central government.

Out of these unsettled conditions, Gabriel García Moreno—a conservative leader with strong ties to the Roman Catholic Church—rose to power. Either directly through the presidency or indirectly through personal influence, García Moreno controlled Ecuador's fortunes between 1860 and 1875. Using the landed aristocracy and the Church as his power base, García Moreno turned his energies to reorganizing the nation. By ignoring the Constitution of 1861, which decentralized power, the president initiated many programs. His agenda included increasing agricultural production, building railroads and highways, developing foreign trade, and stimulating industry. These advances, however, were achieved at the expense of the personal freedom of Ecuador's citizens. Political disagreement was not allowed, and education came under the sole authority of the Church. Indeed, the 1869 Constitution stated that only practicing Catholics qualified for citizenship.

Despite attempts to stamp out liberal sentiments, particularly those that clearly separated Church and state, a strong anti-García Moreno movement developed. The movement ended with the assassination of the president on the steps of the executive residence in 1875.

The following 20 years were violent. Conservative *serranos* (highlanders), most of whom were Catholic landowners of large estates in the sierra, tried to maintain control over Ecuadoran politics. But Guayaquil's liberal *costeños* (lowlanders), enriched by Ecuador's growing international connections, continued to gain power. Finally, in 1895 General Eloy Alfaro, leader of the Guayaquil liberals, won control of the government in a revolutionary coup d'état. Later he was elected president under the new Constitution of 1897.

Photo by Organization of American States

The liberal policies of Eloy Alfaro *(above)* largely undid the preferential treatment given to the Roman Catholic Church by Gabriel García Moreno.

The Twentieth Century

Liberalism thrived under the administrations of Eloy Alfaro and his hand-picked successor, General Leónidas Plaza Gutiérrez, who governed Ecuador from 1901 to 1905. Church and state were separated, and education was removed from Catholic control. Divorce laws were passed, civil registration of marriage was required, and freedom of the press and of religion were

Photo by Organization of American States

As this 1910 street scene indicates, Ecuadorans benefited from governmental improvements that brought electricity to public buildings and paved main streets during the more liberal regimes of Alfaro and Plaza Gutiérrez.

guaranteed. All Church-owned property that was not used directly for religious purposes was taken away. The government took control of the large estates. Improvements were made in health, education, transportation, and the operation of public utilities. In 1906 Ecuadorans celebrated the completion of the Guayaquil-Quito Railroad, an impressive but costly feat of engineering.

Rivalry between Alfaro and Plaza caused considerable civil disruption between 1906 and 1912. A final confrontation ended in the death of Alfaro and the reestablishment of Plaza as chief executive. Upon his return to power in 1912, Plaza continued his earlier progressive administration. Though he began reforms in education and authorized work on new railway lines, Plaza realized that Ecuador was heavily in debt. The nation's chief creditor was the Commercial and Agricultural Bank of Guayaquil, which had grown wealthy by investing in the development of the sugar, petroleum, and manufacturing industries. The bankers replaced the Roman Catholic Church as Ecuador's most powerful nongovernmental group.

The global depression of the 1930s found Ecuador, like countries elsewhere, wrestling with severe social and economic problems. These difficulties led to polarization between liberal and conservative political groups, as factions and new parties rallied around the personalities of popular leaders. On the national level, presidents, provisional presidents, dictators, and military juntas replaced one another in rapid succession. None had enough time in office to build strong national agreement on a course of action to confront Ecuador's problems.

During the 1930s and 1940s, Ecuadoran politics were volatile and often self-defeating. Taking advantage of the unsettled situation in 1941, Peruvian troops entered

Courtesy of Minneapolis Public Library and Information Center

With the encouragement of President Galo Plaza Lasso—an expert in mechanized agriculture—Ecuador capitalized on the banana blight that had ruined crops in the nations of Central America. By 1952—the end of Plaza's term of office—Ecuador's plantations were exporting record amounts of this crop.

Recurring political problems plagued the administration of Galo Plaza. Yet as president he significantly furthered Ecuador's agricultural development and introduced a measure of economic prosperity.

Courtesy of Organization of American States

Ecuador to recover lands of disputed ownership and defeated Ecuadoran forces after a month of intense fighting. When the matter was finally resolved by foreign ministers who met in Rio de Janeiro in 1942, Ecuador had lost 72,000 square miles of El Oriente territory to Peru. Recovery of that lost territory remains a goal of Ecuador's foreign policy.

The election of Galo Plaza Lasso in 1948 ushered in a period of progressive rule and improved economic fortunes for Ecuador. Plaza, a civilian, was the son of former president Leónidas Plaza. The younger Plaza had been educated in the United States and returned to Ecuador as a practical farmer and an authority on dairy cattle breeding. Plaza became the first chief executive since 1924 to complete the four-year presidential term decreed by the constitution.

Plaza presided over a democratic administration that respected individual freedoms and that allowed the free flow of information. As president, he undertook vigorous programs to improve crop and livestock raising and to safeguard the land through soil conservation. His administration urged highlanders to move out of the thickly populated sierra to the lesser-populated lowlands. When a banana disease wiped out plantings in Central America, Plaza moved quickly to support the development of banana production in Ecuador. During Plaza's term of office, Ecuador became the world's main banana exporter.

The Political Scene Since the 1950s

Though Plaza's regime showed marked signs of progress, it is not representative of the turbulent history of Ecuadoran politics. The leadership style of José María Velasco Ibarra—the president who preceded and succeeded Plaza—is a better example of the ups and downs of governing Ecuador. Beginning in 1934, Velasco Ibarra served as president five times and was thrown out of office four times, usually by a military coup d'état. Repeatedly elected by the urban masses, Velasco Ibarra made rousing speeches that appealed to the poor. Once in office, he alienated even his friends by his unpredictable actions. Moreover, Velasco Ibarra seldom was able to design a sensible program that satisfied the hopes he aroused while campaigning for office.

When Velasco Ibarra was reelected in 1952 to succeed Plaza, Ecuador was enjoying economic growth. The new regime survived by following the blueprints laid out by the Plaza administration and by adhering to the controls imposed by the Central Bank of Ecuador and the Monetary Board. Railway- and road-building programs went forward, Ecuador's foreign trade increased, and the government was able to balance its financial books. Prevented by the constitution from immediate reelection, Velasco Ibarra completed his term and handed over power to Camilo Ponce Enríquez, the third president in a row to take office peacefully and constitutionally.

Velasco Ibarra spent most of the next four years living abroad. He returned in 1960 to win election to a fourth term as president by a large majority of votes. In his inaugural address, Velasco Ibarra denounced the so-called Rio Protocol—the unpopular 1942 settlement of hostilities

Courtesy of Organization of American States

Velasco Ibarra served as president five times between 1934 and 1972. Skilled in the handling of crowds and a gifted orator, Velasco Ibarra was deposed four times while in office. Although he often censored the press, his governments encouraged the construction of new roads and schools.

Courtesy of Earl H. Lubensky

Surrounded by the military—who would later remove Velasco Ibarra from office—the resilient president parades through the streets of Guayaquil in the early 1970s, acknowledging the response of the crowd with a raised hand.

with Peru—under which Ecuador lost so much of its territory. When he expressed sympathy for the Communist regime of Fidel Castro in Cuba, however, he separated himself from conservative military officers. A worsening economic situation soon forced Velasco Ibarra to resign.

An extended period of military rule followed. It ended in 1968 with the election of Velasco Ibarra to a fifth presidential term of office. To cope with a steadily declining economy, widespread public protest, and student riots, Velasco Ibarra suspended the constitution and dissolved the congress in 1970. Initially, Ecuador's military leadership supported these drastic actions. But by 1972 Velasco Ibarra's policies had enraged the military to such an extent that—for the fourth time—a military junta forced him from office. A succession of provisional military regimes followed, and new elections were finally held in 1979.

Throughout the 1980s, Ecuador's civilian presidents encountered violence and social turmoil. Ecuadoran leaders also struggled with a weak economy and a sharp drop in oil earnings. Sixto Durán Ballén, who became Ecuador's president in 1992, began a campaign of privatization, in which state-owned companies were sold to foreign investors.

Political corruption and turmoil continued to distract Ecuadorans from economic issues in the late 1990s. In 1997 the legislature deposed President Abdalá Bucaram for corruption after several days of public protests against Bucaram's rule. The chairman of the congress, Fabián Alarcón, became interim president until a national presidential election could be held in mid-1998. At the same time, voters prepared to elect a constituent assembly that will rewrite Ecuador's constitution and reform a weak and widely distrusted government.

Government

Ecuador's constitution of 1979 provides for a republican form of government, with a chief executive, a unicameral (one-house) legislature, and a supreme court. Voting is compulsory for every Ecuadoran citizen who can read and write and who is over 18 years of age. The nonliterate population may also vote but is not obliged to do so.

In accordance with constitutional amendments approved in 1983, the president is elected by direct vote to a four-year term. The president, who may not serve consecutive terms, appoints a 16-member cabinet, the governors of provinces, and other administrative employees.

Ecuador's congress meets in full session only two months out of every year beginning on August 10. The congress also has four full-time committees to consider legislation when the congress is in recess. Seventy deputies are elected to two-year terms from lists of candidates drawn up in the various provinces by legally recognized parties. Twelve deputies are elected on a national basis and serve four-year terms.

Ecuador's highest court is comprised of a president and 30 justices who serve four-year terms and are appointed by the congress. The power to review the acts of government also rests with Ecuador's high court.

Courtesy of Embassy of Ecuador, Washington, D.C.

After his election in 1992, President Sixto Durán Ballén attempted a series of difficult economic reforms. Public protests against these measures broke out in Quito in the fall of 1992. Ballén's successor, Abdalá Bucaram, also saw violent protests against his administration and was forced out of office by a vote of the Ecuadoran congress.

In the town of Coca, a woman washes herself and her young child in the Napo River.

Courtesy of Leonard Soroka

3) The People

The population of Ecuador is about 12 million and is growing at the rapid rate of 2.3 percent a year. The government has launched a vast development plan to improve housing, welfare, education, agriculture, transportation, and manufacturing. About 40 percent of the people still live in rural areas. The provinces of Guayas, Manabí, and Pichincha have the greatest concentrations of rural families.

Ethnic Groups

Mestizos—those of mixed Indian-and-European bloodlines—and pure Indians represent respectively 55 and 25 percent of

Ecuador's ethnic mixture. Approximately 10 percent of Ecuador's population is of pure European—mostly Spanish—origin. Blacks, who live mainly along the coast, make up the remaining 10 percent.

Indians in rural areas often speak languages other than Spanish, primarily Quechua and Jivaroan. Urban mestizos usually speak Spanish, the nation's official language. Many live in the cities and take part in a Spanish-style society. In rural areas, mestizos often adopt Indian patterns of living.

THE INDIANS

Of the once-numerous tribes of the costa, few Indian groups remain. Only the Colorado and the Cayapa have retained separate cultural identities. Both groups are related to Colombia's Chibcha but speak different languages and have different traditions from one another. Most Colorado and Cayapa are farmers.

In El Oriente Indians belong to several major groups, including the Yumbo, Jivaro, and Auca. The Yumbo are a Quechua-speaking tribe who live along the banks of

Courtesy of World Bank

An Indian woman harvests potatoes at an Andean farm along the main road to Latacunga.

Independent Picture Service

Indians of El Oriente preserve their traditional lifestyles despite the surrounding modern world. Their houses are still fashioned of upright bamboo poles, and their clothing continues to be appropriate for the hot, humid climate in which they live.

the many rivers that flow through El Oriente. The tribe is a mixture of many peoples who became disunited with the coming of the Spaniards. By adopting one language—Quechua—and by remaining isolated, the Yumbo have been able to forge a new tribal identity from different elements.

The Jivaro occupy the provinces of Morona-Santiago, Zamora-Chinchipe, and Pastaza near the Peruvian border. Once renowned as headhunters, the Jivaro have largely rejected Western contact. They speak their own language—Jivaroan—but also know Quechua through contact with other tribes of El Oriente. Along with the smaller Auca tribe, the Jivaro represent peoples who have preserved their culture, religious beliefs, traditions, and language since pre-Columbian times.

The Otavalo Indians, who live northeast of Quito in the province of Imbabura, perhaps have had more contact with Western influences than any other Ecuadoran native group. They are famous for the excellence of their handwoven textiles, which they market nationwide and beyond. Despite widespread contact with non-Indians, the Otavalo maintain a strong cultural identity and set of traditions.

Courtesy of Evangeline Quam

The textiles of the Otavalo Indians are well known for their distinctive weave, bright colors, and sharp depiction of the Ecuadoran landscape.

Ecuador's Indian population, long ignored by the government, has demanded to be

Independent Picture Service

On Saturday mornings the Otavalo woolen market draws huge crowds of buyers and sellers. Now highly modernized (the stalls have been removed), the market has grown from a small display of natively produced goods to one of Ecuador's main tourist attractions.

recognized at the national level. In the early 1990s, Indians called for the redistribution of large landholdings. In 1992 the government responded by granting Ecuadoran Indians title to a large tract of land in Pastaza province, in El Oriente.

SMALLER GROUPS

As in many Latin American countries, the small minority of Ecuadorans of pure Spanish descent has had a disproportionate amount of influence on the economic, political, and social life of the nation. Most politicians, wealthy businesspeople, and large landowners come from this group, though there are still considerable differences between the elite of the sierra and of the costa. Tensions between the elite minority and the larger sections of society have brought about political upheavals and have even inspired artistic movements. In contrast, the equally small black population has remained where its forebears landed. On the Ecuadoran coast, where slaves were once imported to work on the coastal sugar plantations, most blacks are farmers. Some, however, are employed as laborers on fishing or cargo boats.

Religion

Today no belief system is officially recognized or given financial support by the Ecuadoran government. Nevertheless, Roman Catholicism has been the dominant religion in Ecuador since the Spanish conquest. The Catholic Church has also been a frequent participant in Ecuadoran politics. Some 95 percent of the people consider themselves Catholic, but few practice the religion. Coastal and highland Indians have been baptized but are Catholic only in a formal sense. In spite of missionary efforts, most El Oriente Indians continue to practice their ancient religions. Although the number of Protestants is growing, the group still makes up less than 1 percent of the population.

Photo by William Gualtieri

Wearing purple clothing to symbolize sorrow, children reenact the journey of Jesus to his crucifixion during a Quito Easter celebration.

Festivals

Fondness for tradition has preserved so many ceremonial rites that festivals are celebrated every month of the year in Ecuador. On Año Viejo, the last night of the year, dolls stuffed with rags, fireworks, and eucalyptus branches are burned at midnight. Many of these figures are humorous representations of political leaders. Some of the revelers are disguised as black-clad widows who beg for money to pay fiesta expenses.

The town of Ambato celebrates its Fair of Fruits and Flowers in February with bullfights, soccer games, parades, dancing in the parks, and exhibits of art and industry. The anniversary of the Battle of Pichincha, on May 24, commemorates Ecuador's independence as a nation.

Courtesy of Earl H. Lubensky

Quito vendors offer colorful masks for sale during Año Viejo—a new Years' Eve festival celebrated throughout Ecuador.

Courtesy of Earl H. Lubensky

Resplendent in their royal robes, children dressed as the three kings—or magi—ride along the new road to Santo Domingo at Christmastime.

Quito holds a fair in the first week of December that celebrates the founding of the capital city. Donkey caravans loaded with fine handicrafts pour in from every province, since the fair has become a showcase for homemade Ecuadoran goods. The days and nights are filled with dances, contests, parties, bullfights, and parades.

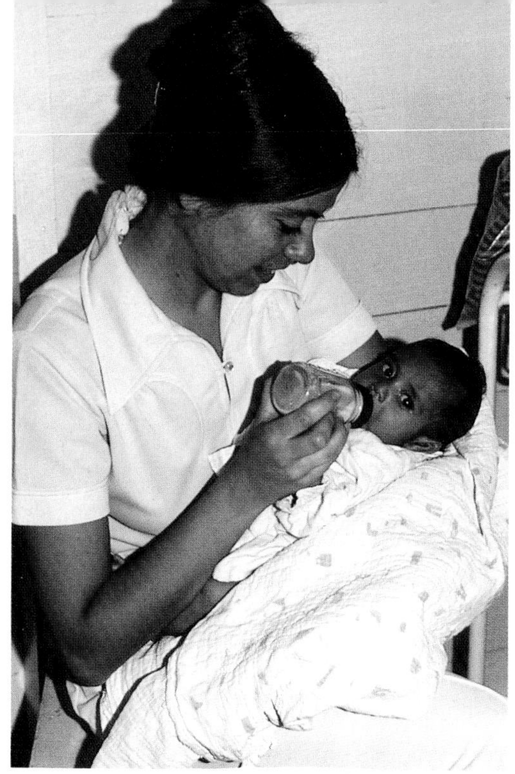

Courtesy of Jeannine Bayard

Ecuador's infant mortality rate has steadily improved in the 1990s but in 1997 was still nearly six times higher than the average for North America.

Health

Health standards are still relatively low, with life expectancy at about 69 years of age. In rural areas, governmental neglect in providing proper sewer and water systems has caused unsanitary living conditions. The scarcity of roads to establish new farms has contributed to malnutrition. Consequently, the diet of impoverished Ecuadorans is deficient in proteins and minerals. Foods like eggs, milk, and vegetables are often too expensive for farmers of small acreages to buy.

Courtesy of Inter-American Development Bank

The lack of sewage and drainage systems in Guayaquil's slums causes untold health problems. Moreover, houses are crowded—thirteen people share the corrugated dwelling in the background.

Courtesy of Leonard Soroka

Children between the ages of 6 and 14 must attend school, but many drop out before completing their primary education. Moreover, school attendance is markedly lower in rural areas than in the cities.

Typhus, typhoid, malaria, yellow fever, and tuberculosis are recurring diseases in Ecuador. While there are good doctors in large cities, medical attention and hospital facilities are still lacking for many Ecuadorans in rural areas.

International and national efforts are in progress to improve health care in Ecuador. The World Health Organization has helped to conduct nationwide vaccination campaigns to prevent disease. The United Nations Children's Fund contributed money to build a large pasteurization plant in Quito, with the provision that part of the milk would be given away at no cost. The infant mortality rate has reached 40 deaths in every 1,000 live births—an average ratio in Latin America.

Education

Despite strides in providing public education, Ecuador is finding it difficult to keep up with its fast-growing population and to make schools available throughout its varied national territory. Education is the single largest item in the national budget and consumes about 25 percent of the nation's annual expenses. By law, education is free and compulsory for all children between the ages of 6 and 14.

Today, with hundreds of new schools in operation, about 76 percent of the children in cities are attending classes. The figure drops to 33 percent, however, in rural areas.

The Ecuadoran government undertook a massive campaign in 1944 to combat illiteracy. The campaign has proved effective, since in the mid-1990s about 90 percent of Ecuador's adults can read and write. Many of them learned these basic skills through educational television.

The two main institutions of higher learning in Quito are the Central University of Ecuador and the Pontifical Catholic

University. Of equal standing with Quito's schools are the University of Cuenca and the State University of Guayaquil.

Food

Many Ecuadorans favor fried foods and *coladas*—meat or vegetable soups thickened with flour that taste slightly sweet. *Locro* is a stew made from cheese and potatoes, and *llapingacho*—a fried pancake made of the same ingredients—is usually topped with egg or avocado. *Ají* is a spicy sauce of hot red peppers, tomatoes, and onions, which is poured over coladas, chicken, or plain rice. *Humitas* (sweet corn tamales), empanadas (meat-filled pastries), and *choclos* (ears of corn toasted in fat) are often sold along the roadside. Seviche, fish delicately marinated in lemon or lime juice, is a popular appetizer.

Courtesy of Earl H. Lubensky

These small children love the taste of *helados*–ice cream–available from a Guayaquil street vendor.

Sports

Ecuador shares with most of Latin America a devotion to soccer, called *futbol,* as the most-popular sport. Professional and amateur teams play in stadiums throughout the country, and informal games are often organized in villages and towns. Another popular sport is *pelota de guante* (glove ball). The sport, which is similar to handball, is played almost exclusively in Ecuador. Participants wear gloves that are attached to round, flat wooden paddles. With these gloves, players hit a heavy rubber ball to each other.

Bullfights are scheduled at least twice each year in Ecuador, usually to coincide with important national festivals, such as Quito's fair in December. Internationally known matadors—mostly from Spain and Mexico—are featured performers.

Independent Picture Service

Players of *pelota de guante* use large, spiked paddles to hit a two-pound ball back and forth to one another.

Courtesy of Museum of Modern Art of Latin America

Soccer—called *futbol* throughout Spanish-speaking countries—is Ecuador's national sport. Matches are often played at Quito's Atahualpa Stadium.

Courtesy of Earl H. Lubensky

Although bullfighting has ancient origins, its modern form derives from Spanish practices of the eighteenth century. In Quito bullfights are part of the celebrations in the first week of December that honor the founding of the capital.

Literature

Ecuadoran literature of the colonial period —like its architecture—is ornate in style. But later creative thought brought in a simpler, nationalist spirit. One of Latin America's first neoclassical poets, José Joaquín Olmedo, played an active role in Ecuador's struggle for independence. Another Ecuadoran, Juan Montalvo, is best remembered for his political essays that attacked Gabriel García Moreno. The classic Ecuadoran novel, *Cumandá*, written by Juan León Merá Martínez, is set in an Indian village at the time of independence and has an Indian girl as its main character.

The twentieth century ushered in a nationalist literary movement throughout South America. Many early Ecuadoran writers—especially those of the sierra—participated in *indigenismo*, a continent-wide style that emphasized pride in pre-Columbian cultures and cursed the exploitation of the native populations. More recent styles have focused on other social protests and on the reawakening of a national Ecuadoran identity.

Jorge Icaza's novel *Huasipungo* is representative of the indigenismo movement.

Courtesy of Museum of Modern Art of Latin America

The natural beauties of Ecuador – including Mount Chimborazo, the nation's highest peak – have inspired many Ecuadoran writers and poets.

Courtesy of Museum of Modern Art of Latin America

Hard-working Andean farmers – who barely grow enough to live on in the rocky, sloping soil – have become the focus of Ecuadoran literature in recent times.

The story focuses on an Indian who labors tirelessly on a small piece of land belonging to a large Andean estate. By exposing the evils of tenant farming—called *huasipungo* in Ecuador—Icaza elevated the Indian to a national symbol of simple virtues and strong faith.

Characteristic of the nationalist spirit are the works of Jorge Carrera Andrade and Gonzalo Escudero. Their poetry de-emphasizes traditional poetic forms in favor of simple landscape images that glorify the beauty of Ecuador.

Courtesy of Museum of Modern Art of Latin America

Intricately worked columns—part of the facade of the church of La Compañía in Quito—reflect the influence of Spain on seventeenth-century Ecuadoran art.

Music

Native Ecuadoran music, much of which began as the ritual music of pre-Columbian Indians, is frequently melancholy. While some ancient tunes have been lost, those that remain preserve their purity, especially in certain Andean regions. Based on the five-tone scale used in the Orient, this music is played on traditional instruments like the quena (a clay or bamboo flute), *pincilla* (a vertical flute), and *rondador* (a panpipe made from a series of bamboo reeds). The peoples of El Oriente devise percussion instruments out of toucan beaks, seed-filled gourds, and hollow logs covered with animal hides.

Independent Picture Service

Native music and elaborate clothing are vital parts of traditional Indian dances.

Instruments introduced by the Spanish include the harp, guitar, and violin. South American composers have combined Indian and Spanish music to produce *música mestiza.* For example, the *yaraví,* an Andean Indian ballad, uses the five-tone scale. The *tonada,* a Spanish variation of the same tune, uses a seven-tone scale, which produces a livelier melody.

Ecuador opened its national conservatory of music in 1870. The first director, Antonio Neumanne, composed the country's national anthem. Today classically trained Ecuadoran musicians blend folk melodies into their compositions. Domenico Brescia included Indian tunes in his *Ecuadoran Symphony.* Segundo Luis Moreno, author of a classic book on Ecuadoran music, also used native rhythms in his *Three Ecuadoran Suites.* Indian influences are also part of Luis Humberto Salgado's symphonic suite entitled *Atahualpa*.

Painting and Sculpture

Quito has been an important art center since colonial times, and its religious art is famous all over the world. A fusion of Indian and Spanish culture—called the Quito school—emerged in the capital and reached its full splendor during the seventeenth century.

The same nationalist sentiments that have inspired writers of poetry and fiction have influenced twentieth-century painters and sculptors. The indigenismo movement found great expression in the murals of Mexican artists, and these works greatly motivated Ecuadoran painters. Oswaldo Guayasamín stands out as the most important advocate of indigenismo. His works depict Indians, mestizos, and blacks in scenes of everyday life. Other muralists, such as Camilo Egas and Eduardo Kingman, use strong, rich colors and simplicity of design to achieve an overall strength of composition—particularly in the illustration of Andean peoples.

Photo by Organization of American States

Color and line combine to bring vitality to Eduardo Kingman's depiction of an Andean woman. Born in Loja, Ecuador, in 1913, Kingman was at the forefront of the twentieth-century *indigenismo* movement.

Oil changed Ecuador's export potential, but many of the nation's inhabitants still earn their living and feed their families by working small, often-rocky parcels of land.

Courtesy of Leonard Soroka

4) The Economy

Ecuador is a small country with a large variety of natural resources, yet it remains one of the most underdeveloped nations in South America. This situation is partly because more than half of its people are subsistence farmers who raise only enough food to feed their families. A high birthrate and inadequate transportation facilities have also kept Ecuador's standard of living low and its annual per capita income below $1,500.

Ecuador's sierra and costa show noticeable economic differences. The sierra lacks agricultural land for expanded farm production and suffers from a surplus of unskilled workers. In contrast, both the costa and El Oriente have abundant land but an insufficient labor force to develop their resources.

Bananas, coffee, cacao, and petroleum exports are crucial to the Ecuadoran economy. Since all of these exports are subject to world competition and price fluctuations, Ecuador's economy often depends on factors beyond its control.

Agriculture and Livestock

Although farming is a major economic activity, less than 20 percent of Ecuador's land is under cultivation. While efforts are being made to diversify farm production, progress is slow. Geographic obstacles and a shortage of cropland in the highlands—where most Ecuadorans live—have hampered development.

Major highland crops are beans, maize, wheat, barley, and potatoes, all of which are grown for domestic consumption.

Courtesy of Leonard Soroka

On large plantations, workers grind the cut stalks of sugarcane by machine before the crop is subjected to further refining.

Courtesy of Inter-American Development Bank

A machine harvests wheat on a farm near Babahoyo, not far from Guayaquil. In recent years agriculture has been modernized in this region.

Independent Picture Service

A woman sorts through drying cacao beans, which come from the gourdlike fruit of the cacao tree.

Independent Picture Service

Banana cutters harvest the fruit from a tall plant on a plantation in Los Ríos province.

Independent Picture Service

A workman carefully examines a stand of maize—a major highland crop.

Photo by William Gualtieri

Indians pick through their potato crop, which will be an important part of their staple diet in the coming year.

Coffee beans are spread out to dry on a large, empty patch of ground in front of a stand of banana plants.

Pyrethrum—a natural insecticide derived from chrysanthemum flowers—is an important cash crop that was developed for export to foreign countries.

Much of the land in the sierra suffers from centuries of constant use as well as from wind and water erosion. In contrast, lowland soils are much better, and coastal farming is geared largely to the export market. Most cacao—from which chocolate is made—is produced on plantations of more than 150 acres, while rice, coffee, and bananas are cultivated mainly on small landholdings by independent farmers. Other lowland crops are yucca, cotton, peanuts, indigo, sugarcane, tobacco, and numerous tropical fruits. Tea plantations have been introduced in El Oriente, along with a factory to process the raw tea.

After a cacao blight in 1933, rice and coffee became Ecuador's major exports. Bananas took the lead when plant diseases destroyed the Central American banana

Courtesy of Inter-American Development Bank

Near Daule, a farmer plants part of his rice crop in a well-irrigated section of his land. In Ecuador–as in most of Latin America–the planting and harvesting of rice is done by hand.

crop. While Ecuador is still among the world's chief exporters of bananas, it again faces competition from Central America. Ecuadoran banana shippers must constantly look for new markets and introduce new methods of packing. Today coffee and bananas are Ecuador's largest agricultural exports. The country is growing more and more rice, which is eaten as a substitute for expensive, imported wheat.

Ecuador also is a leading producer of abaca. Introduced in the late 1930s, this plant produces a hard vegetable fiber used in making twine, mats, surgical clothing, disposable diapers, and high-quality paper. Ninety percent of the harvest is shipped to the United States—the world's largest importer of abaca.

Ecuador's dairy industry is located in the irrigated highland plateau that extends from Ibarra to Riobamba. About two million sheep graze in the highlands. Though their wool is of poor quality, their meat is delicious. While previously livestock were raised only for home consumption, today cattle and pig raising are

Courtesy of Laurie Nelsen

Highland families raise top-grade sheep wherever there is good pastureland.

Courtesy of Earl H. Lubensky

Rows of fat, slaughtered pigs reflect Ecuador's developing interest in the livestock industry.

Courtesy of Earl H. Lubensky

A crew pulls in their nets along Ecuador's Pacific coast. The fishermen hope for a good catch of anchovies, fish found off the coast of the Santa Elena Peninsula.

Photo by Robert E. Olson

A man and his young helper wash freshly caught crabs to prepare them for market.

sizable industries. The country has begun to export some of its meat products.

Fishing and Forestry

Ecuador's coastal waters provide a rich fishing ground. Annual catches reached 300,000 tons in the 1980s, but fell sharply after a warm ocean current known as El Niño killed off a high proportion of plankton, the microscopic food that small fish eat. By the late 1990s, shrimp fishing had recovered and was providing one of Ecuador's leading exports. The country claims exclusive fishing rights to ocean waters within 200 miles of Ecuador's coastline.

The timber covering more than three-quarters of Ecuador is one of the nation's greatest untapped natural resources. Virgin forest covers about 10,000 square miles on the Pacific coast—extending from the sea to an altitude of 5,000 feet in the Andes. An additional 80,000 square miles

Courtesy of John H. Peck

Trucks haul out hardwood logs that have been cut down in the acres of forested land throughout Ecuador.

lie in the Amazon Basin east of the Andes. The vast tropical jungle contains more than 2,000 different kinds of trees, including valuable cedar, walnut, redwood, and brazilwood, but the rugged terrain makes the trees difficult to harvest. Ecuador is the world's largest exporter of balsa—the lightest wood in the world. Fast-growing eucalyptus trees provide both fuel and useful building material in the sierra. More than 90 percent of the wood cut in Ecuador is burned for fuel, particularly in the highlands where it is often cold at night.

Independent Picture Service

Balsa wood is so light that one person can easily carry an entire log, as demonstrated by a sawmill worker.

Courtesy of Earl H. Lubensky

Before vast deposits of oil were discovered in El Oriente, workers pumped petroleum by hand along the Santa Elena Peninsula, where the oil was very near the surface.

Courtesy of Earl H. Lubensky

This petroleum refinery operated well in advance of the oil boom of the 1970s. The plant converted crude petroleum into gasoline, naphtha, and kerosene.

Courtesy of Earl H. Lubensky

The powdery remains of ground sugarcane stalks—called bagasse—are used at this refinery in Milagro to fuel the furnaces.

Mining and Industry

Although some salt, gold, silver, sulfur, gypsum, copper, lignite (brown coal), and kaolin (clay used in ceramics) are mined, petroleum is still Ecuador's major mining industry. In 1972 a pipeline began carrying crude oil across the Andes to the coast for refinement and export. The country's oil wells produced more than 386,000 barrels a day during the mid-1990s. Ecuador is the second largest oil exporter in Latin America, after Venezuela.

Petroecuador, the state oil company, grants leases to foreign oil companies and collects royalties on petroleum exports. In the mid-1990s, oil contributed about 40 percent of Ecuador's export earnings and paid for more than 60 percent of the state budget. Nevertheless, the government plans to sell shares in Petroecuador to private investors.

Industrial development in Ecuador is restricted by the country's small domestic market and by its lack of skilled workers.

Courtesy of Evangeline Quam

Craftspeople use hand-dyed wool in the production of woven textiles.

Independent Picture Service

The shipbuilding industry has increased as part of the growth of Guayaquil's port facilities.

An Indian worker painstakingly chips away at huge blocks of limestone, which will be used to make cement.

Independent Picture Service

Independent Picture Service

Ecuador's wealth of forest resources has resulted in the popularity of furniture making as a profession.

Manufacturing accounts for about 25 percent of Ecuador's total production. Food processing is the most important part of the manufacturing sector. Other major industries produce shoes, clothes, textiles, furniture, and building supplies. Sugar and flour mills and fertilizer plants are also becoming major industries.

Recent revisions in Ecuador's laws have enabled foreign companies to offer technical assistance and new credit. By lowering taxes on certain businesses, the government has also encouraged investment in manufacturing. The Andean Group, a subregional common market, has created a multinational development bank to help finance industrial investments in all Andean nations.

Courtesy of Inter-American Development Bank

Ecuadoran and Italian engineers collaborated to build the hydroelectricity station on the Paute River. The plant serves the energy needs of Cuenca, about 60 miles away.

Energy

While Ecuador's hydroelectric potential is impressive, little of it has been harnessed.

Courtesy of Earl H. Lubensky

Bags of charcoal piled along the roadside between Quito and Santo Domingo await delivery trucks that will carry them to metropolitan markets.

Currently, about 22 percent of the nation's electricity comes from hydropower. The remainder comes mostly from thermal plants that burn coal or petroleum. Due to shortages of electrical power, many factories have installed their own generating plants. Only half of Ecuador's people have electrical service, and the systems in larger towns are frequently overloaded. Most utility plants are locally owned, although there is a large, privately owned company in Guayaquil.

Electrical capacity has increased greatly in recent decades, but demand still far exceeds supply. The government has established the Ecuadoran Institute of Electrification to coordinate production and distribution of electrical power.

Courtesy of Earl H. Lubensky

Near Cumbayá outside Quito, pipelines send hydroelectrically generated power to the capital.

Courtesy of Leonard Soroka

The Agoyan dam near the town of Baños takes its power from the Pastaza River and supplies energy to central Ecuador.

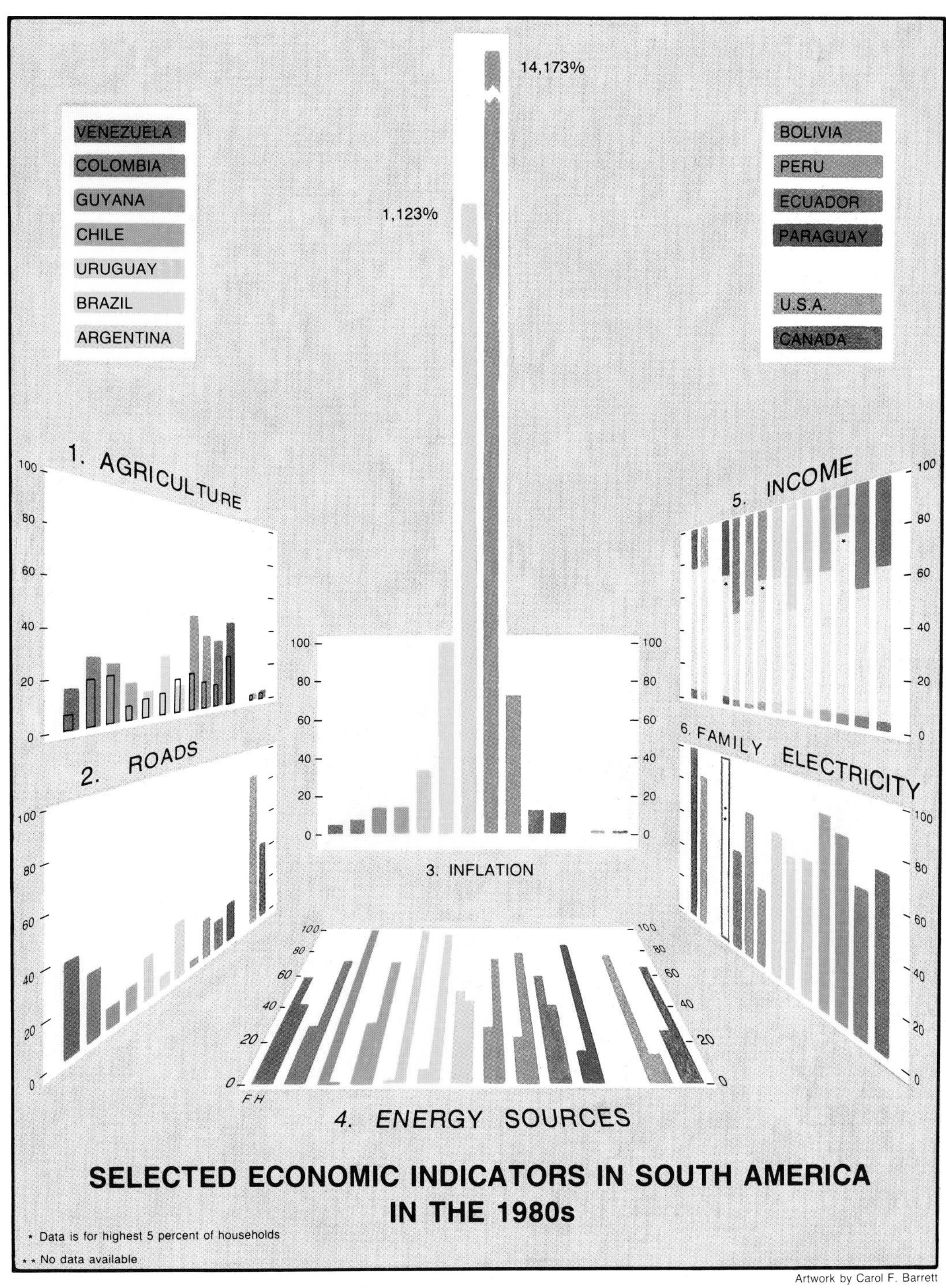

Artwork by Carol F. Barrett

This multigraph depicts six important South American economic factors. The same factors for the United States and Canada are included for comparison. Data is from *1986 Britannica Book of the Year, Encyclopedia of the Third World, Europa Yearbook,* and *Countries of the World and their Leaders, 1987.*

In GRAPH 1—labeled Agriculture—the colored bars show the percentage of a country's total labor force that works in agriculture. The overlaid black boxes show the percentage of a country's gross domestic product that comes from agriculture. In most cases—except Argentina —the number of agricultural workers far exceeds the amount of income produced by the farming industry.

GRAPH 2 depicts the percentage of paved roads, while GRAPH 3 illustrates the inflation rate. The inflation figures for Colombia, Guyana, and Brazil are estimated. GRAPH 4 depicts two aspects of energy usage. The left half of a country's bar is the percentage of energy from fossil fuel (oil or coal); the right half shows the percentage of energy from hydropower. In GRAPH 5, which depicts distribution of wealth, each country's bar represents 100 percent of its total income. The top section is the portion of income received by the richest 10 percent of the population. The bottom section is the portion received by the poorest 20 percent. GRAPH 6 represents the percentage of homes that have electricity.

Courtesy of Jeannine Bayard

In the Ecuadoran jungle, heavy rains turned a once-passable road into a sea of mud during the rainy season.

Courtesy of Museum of Modern Art of Latin America

In the rugged Andes, where few paved roads exist, many people travel on horseback.

Transportation

Heavy rainfall, rugged mountains, and dense forests have hindered the development of transportation facilities. The Guayaquil-Quito Railroad, begun in 1897, was completed after nine difficult years. Single-track rail lines now connect major cities. Nevertheless, in 1983 heavy rains destroyed much of the track between Guayaquil and Cuenca and forced the temporary cancellation of many trains. Belgian-German financing was arranged for railway rebuilding and modernization.

Buses also travel between most cities. Some buses are owned individually and some by cooperatives. Ecuador now has several thousand miles of all-weather highway and many paved secondary roads. The Pan-American Highway extends north to south through the sierra. Another main road is under construction across the coastal plain and will link Machala in the southwest with Esmeraldas in the northwest. It will also be tied into the Pan-American Highway and into Quito. Experts are studying the possibility of building a north-south highway along the edge of El Oriente jungle, east of the Andes.

Courtesy of Inter-American Development Bank

A section of the Pan-American Highway near Cayambe is dwarfed by the towering peak of Mount Chimborazo. This major international highway is essential to the flow of South America's commercial traffic.

Courtesy of Leonard Soroka

No bridges span the Coca River, and this bus must be ferried across the waterway to continue along its scheduled route.

Due to its rugged terrain, air transportation is vitally important to Ecuador. In addition to modern international jet airports at Quito and Guayaquil, many smaller towns have airports. Weather conditions at Quito's high altitude prohibit night flying in the capital.

The Future

After the boom years of the 1970s, Ecuador suffered a sharp economic downturn, as the price of oil—the country's most important export—fell. Coupled with this drop was a decline in Ecuador's income from its principal agricultural exports—bananas, coffee, and cacao.

To cope with this sudden downturn in the country's fortunes, Ecuadoran authorities devalued the national currency, the sucre. The government also cut spending to match its falling revenues. As a result, programs to develop natural resources and to build new roads lost funding. In an attempt to stem the worsening trade deficit, the authorities also restricted imports to only the most essential items. To meet the demand for banned consumer items, smuggling increased along Ecuador's borders with Colombia and Peru. At the same time, inflation lowered the value of paychecks received by Ecuadoran workers.

Sixto Durán Ballén, who came to power in 1992, attempted to solve the economic problems with difficult reforms. By selling to private investors the 167 state-owned companies, Durán planned to raise cash needed to pay Ecuador's debts. State-employed workers, however, opposed this privatization plan because they feared the loss of their jobs and a decline in their living standards.

Courtesy of John H. Peck

Enjoyment of the spectacular oil wealth of the 1970s has yielded to worries about the worldwide petroleum market. Falling prices reduced Ecuador's oil earnings in the 1980s and 1990s.

Courtesy of Earl H. Lubensky

A demonstration by Ecuadoran Indians suggests that Ecuador has not been able to satisfy the needs of its native population. Visible signs read "Campesinos (rural workers) ask that the small property tax be abandoned," and "The irrigation canal at Atocha Huachi belongs to those who built it—not to the lazy landowners."

Ecuador also must try to resolve its border dispute with Peru, a conflict that has threatened open warfare between the two nations. In January 1995, Ecuadoran and Peruvian soldiers clashed several times along the border. Agreements signed later that year and in 1996 established a demilitarized zone and opened the region, for the first time in many years, to commercial and civilian traffic.

The development of Ecuador's rain forest also poses a difficult problem. New roads and towns are springing up in El Oriente, and foreign companies are eager to exploit the extensive oil resources of the region. But development and oil drilling also threaten environmental damage, and the indigenous peoples of the area are fighting to keep their hold on the land.

Despite these setbacks, Ecuadoran democracy has survived several years of social and economic turmoil. If the government can provide a growing economy, and successfully resolve the thorny issue of oil development, Ecuador has a chance at a brighter future.

Courtesy of John H. Peck

Ecuador may yet be able to harness its vast natural resources—such as its rivers for hydropower—to bring a better standard of living to its citizens.

Index